Clean Break and Royal

Conceived by Stacey Gregg and Deborah Pearson

**Devised with Lucy Edkins, Jennifer Joseph,
TerriAnn Oudjar and Jade Small**

Conceived by Stacey Gregg and Deborah Pearson
Devised with Lucy Edkins, Jennifer Joseph, TerriAnn Oudjar, Jade Small
Assistant Director Milli Bhatia
Designer Camilla Clarke
Choreographer Yassmin V Foster
Lighting Designer Natasha Chivers
Sound Designer Ella Wahlström
Video Artist Edie Morris
Voice Coach Emma Woodvine
Stage Manager on the book Tamsin Withers
Stage Manager on the floor Crystal Gayle
Outside Eye Laura Dannequin

Cast & Creative Team.

Lucy Edkins

Lucy has known of Clean Break since she moved back to London in the mid 90s after a stint up North with Nomads, a theatre and film company she co-founded which worked with vulnerable groups (including prisoners) and performed plays in unconventional venues. She postponed her plan to take off to the States to work in film for a few months, working here as a stage manager on the fringe, during which time she took a few workshops with Clean Break including a Complicité workshop culminating in a devised piece, *The Ex-Industry*, performed in local prisons and a rehab unit. She went on to work professionally with Clean Break in their stage management teams, including on *Mules* and *Yard Gal* at the Royal Court, touring nationally with the latter around prisons and art centres. In the States she worked in Off Broadway theatre and the non-union film sector mainly on the technical side, though continuing to take on bit parts as they came along. Back in the UK she continued to work in theatre, stage managing and as assistant director on *Life After Life* at the National Theatre. Since 2003 she has concentrated on artistic work across media, including a couple of years playwriting and showcasing new works. This is her first professional acting engagement.

Jennifer Joseph

Jennifer has been a Clean Break Member since 2010. After completing her studies and performing in multiple short touring productions with the company, Jen is now a successful actor. She continues to work with Clean Break, speaking about her experiences and performing in the company's work, most recently in *Hear* by Deborah Bruce which was performed at the House of Lords. Between 2014-2016, she acted alongside a stellar cast in Phyllida Lloyd's *Shakespeare Trilogy* for the Donmar Warehouse and continues to find other success both on stage and screen. As a potent advocate for Arts in Prisons, she takes part in outreach programmes about penal issues and is a Trustee of Women In Prison. Her most recent roles include appearances in *Flush* at the Matchstick Theatre, and in the upcoming horror film *Patients of a Saint*, directed by Russell Owen.

TerriAnn Oudjar

TerriAnn has been a Clean Break member since 2004 but has been performing on stage and screen. In 2003 she appeared in BBC2's *Grass*, and in 2004 in BBC3's *Killing Time*. The same year she featured in *Stealing Lives* for Channel 4. TerriAnn has also performed in feature films *Rabbit Fever* (2006) and *Trauma* (2004). In 2016 she appeared in *The Vagina Monologues* on stage at the Bristol Bierkeller and most recently in *Robin Hood: The Arrow of Destiny* at Theatre Peckham. All the while she has performed in, and been Assistant Director on many Clean Break shows, as well as facilitating workshops.

Jade Small

Jade has been a Clean Break Member since 2013. After completing her studies, she won a bursary to The Royal Central School of Speech and Drama and was awarded a Diploma in Acting. In 2014 she starred in *Friendtimacy* by Stacey Gregg: the curtain-raiser for Phyllida Lloyd's critically acclaimed *Henry IV* at The Donmar Warehouse. In 2015 she appeared at The National Theatre, and at Latitude Festival in *Sweatbox* by Chloë Moss, a ground-breaking, immersive piece of theatre performed entirely within a real prison van.

Stacey Gregg

Stacey's credits include: *Lights Out* (The Site Programme); *Nod If You Can Hear Me* (The Big Idea) for the Royal Court, *Scorch* (Prime Cut); *Choices* (Royal Exchange, Manchester/WoW Festival, Southbank/ Dublin Fringe/Outburst); *Override* (Watford Palace/Dublin Fringe); *Shibboleth, Perve* (Abbey, Dublin). Television includes: *The Innocents, Riviera, The Frankenstein Chronicles, Your Ma's a Hard Brexit*. As Performer: *Everything Between Us* (Project Arts Centre); *Moth* (Hightide, the Bush).

Deborah Pearson

Deborah Pearson is an artist, playwright and theatre-maker. Her work has been on in 22 countries on 5 continents and has been translated into 5 languages. She is founder and co-Director of the artist-curator collective Forest Fringe.

Deborah's credits include: *It's All Made Up* (Royal Court/The Site Programme); *History History History* (Théâtre Garonne/bit teatergarasjen, Norway/International tour); *Post National* (Volcano,

Canada); *Made Visible* (Yard); *The Future Show* (BAC/International tour). Television includes: *No Time to Sleep* (Justice Project Pakistan). Visual art includes: *The Filibuster* (Somerset House); *Make Yourself at Home* (Nuit Blanche, Brussels); *Drifting Right* (Next Wave Festival, Melbourne).

Milli Bhatia – Assistant Director

Milli is completing her term as Trainee Director at the Royal Court, where she directed *Shine*. Other theatre includes: *Dismantle This Room, The Hijabi Monologues, My White Best Friend/This Bitter Earth* [part of Black Lives Black Words] (Bush); *I Have AIDS* [Jerwood Assistant Director Programme] (Young Vic); *Rats* (Duffield Studio, National); *Three Wheels On the Wagon* (Birmingham Repertory Theatre); *EmpowerHouse* (Theatre Royal, Stratford East); *No Cowboys Only Indians* (Courtyard). As associate director, other theatre includes: *What if Women Ruled the World?* (Manchester International Festival).

Camilla Clarke – Designer

Camilla is a set and costume designer based in London, UK. She trained at the Royal Welsh College of Music and Drama, graduating in 2014 with First Class Honours in Theatre Design. Her work as designer for the Royal Court includes: *Bad Roads and Human Animals*. Other theatre as designer includes: *Beginners* (Unicorn Theatre); Elephant (Birmingham Rep); *Yuri* (Chapter, Cardiff); *Frogman* (Curious Directive/Traverse); *No Place for a Woman* (503); *Wind Resistance* (Lyceum, Edinburgh); *Seagulls* (Volcano). Her work as Associate Designer includes: *B,* and *Victory Condition.* Awards include: Linbury Prize for Stage Design; Lord Williams Prize for Design; The Prince of Wales Design Scholarship.

Yassmin V Foster – Choreographer

Yassmin is influenced by her heritage and experience of black culture, in particular the artistic expression of dance and music. Yassmin has worked progressively in the arts and culture sector since 1992, and her work has taken her to South and North America, Asia and Europe. Theatre credits include: *Queens of Sheba* by Jessica Hagan, *With A Little Bit of Luck* by Sabrina Mahfouz and *All We Ever Wanted Was Everything* by Luke Barnes.

Natasha Chivers – Lighting Designer

Natasha is a lighting designer based in London with over 20 years' experience for clients including The Bridge Theatre, the Old Vic and the National Theatres of England, Scotland and Wales. Her work for the Royal Court includes: *The Cane, Bad Roads, Adler & Gibb, The Mistress Contract, Gastronauts, The Djinns of Eidgah, That Face* (& West End). Other theatre includes: *Allelujah* (Bridge/NT Live); *Oedipus* (Toneelgroep, Amsterdam); The *Duchess of Malfi* (RSC); *Sylvia* (Old Vic); *1984* (West End/Broadway); *27, The Wolves in the Walls, Home* (National Theatre of Scotland). In 2007 she won an Olivier Award for *Sunday In The Park With George* and in 2016 was nominated for another, one for lighting *Oresteia* at The Almeida.

Ella Wahlström – Sound Designer

Ella Wahlström is a Finnish sound designer. She trained at Rose Bruford College and lives in London. She's the sound designer of Esa-Pekka Salonen's *Cello Concerto* which premiered at Chicago Symphony Orchestra in 2017 with Yo-Yo Ma as the soloist. She's an original sound operator of the multi award-winning *The Encounter* by Simon McBurney/Complicite, and has toured with it internationally including Broadway. She's the co-sound designer of Robert Wilson and Mikhail Baryshnikov's *Letter to a Man* (BAM Harvey, Spoleto festival). Recent theatre sound designs include: *Peter Pan Goes Wrong* (London West End, UK and international tour) *Black&White* (SJACC, Kuwait); *Trying It On* (RSC, Royal Court, UK tour); *Jellyfish* (The Bush); *Of Kith and Kin* (Sheffield Crucible, The Bush); *The Life* (English Theatre Frankfurt).

Edie Morris – Video Artist

Edie studied 'Design for Performance' and graduated from the Royal Welsh College of Music and Drama in 2018. A specialist in video design and animation, Edie produces animation for theatre, film and music, where projects include stop frame animation for music videos. In 2015 Edie created the video for My Bad Sister's video for *Two Tears*. In 2016 she then delivered video design for Pyratix Circus' show *Alice in Wasteland* at the Edinburgh Fringe. In 2018 Edie was Design Assistant for National Theatre Wales' production *Tide Whisperer* and created video design and interactive projection for *English Eccentrics*. Since 2016 Edie has designed the main stage for Nozstock Music Festival in Hertfordshire.

Emma Woodvine – Voice Coach

Emma's previous work as a Voice Coach for the Royal Court includes: *Pigs and dogs; Hang; Routes.* Other theatre work includes: *Fun Home; A Streetcar Named Desire; Happy Days; Scotsboro' Boys; A Season in the Congo; A Doll's House; The Changeling; Beloved; After Miss Julie; I Am Yussef and This Is My Brother* (Young Vic); *Machinal* (Almeida Theatre); *Imperium part I and II; Richard II; Henry IV Parts I and II; Henry V; The Two Gentlemen of Verona; The Witch of Edmonton; Loves Sacrifice; The Jew of Malta* (RSC); *Twelfth Night* (Royal Exchange Manchester); *Happy* Days; *Ghost the Musical* (West End); *The Winter's Tale; 'Tis Pity She's a Whore, Macbeth* (Cheek by Jowl); *The Magic Flute; Kiss Me Kate; Carousel* (Opera North/WNO/Barbican); *Dick Whittington* (Lyric Hammersmith); *Pitchfork Disney* (Arcola); *The School for Scandal; 11 and 12* (Barbican Theatre).

WHO WE ARE

Clean Break is a women's theatre company established by two women prisoners in 1979 at HMP Askham Grange in Yorkshire. For forty years we have used ground-breaking theatre to transform the lives of women with criminal justice experience and challenge preconceptions.

WHAT WE DO

Our award-winning theatre productions share with audiences the often-hidden stories of women and crime. We are proud to have co-produced our new plays with dozens of UK theatres, including the Royal Court Theatre, Manchester Royal Exchange, Birmingham Rep, Theatr Clwyd, The Royal Shakespeare Company and Soho Theatre.

We have engaged with thousands of women on the fringes or with experience of the criminal justice system (our Members) from our women-only building in Kentish Town: a safe space where learning happens, and transformation becomes possible. The programme's success has grown generations of highly skilled and confident alumni, 70% of whom currently progress to further studies, employment or long-term volunteering roles.

"It was a breath of fresh air; it took me out of here and helped me to imagine something better." Participant at HMP Low Newton

Clean Break has been fortunate to work with many extraordinary writers and creative teams over the past forty years. Our commissioning process offers a unique exchange between artists, our Members and women in prison. Many of the artists we work with covet their time with Clean Break and have articulated how formative their time with us has been. Lucy Kirkwood put it like this:

"As an artist my commission with Clean Break has inspired and sustained me creatively in brilliant and unexpected ways." Lucy Kirkwood, Olivier Award Winner and Clean Break Patron

SUPPORT CLEAN BREAK

We can't do it without you. If you'd like to help us use theatre to change lives, please visit our website, **www.cleanbreak.org.uk**

KEEP IN TOUCH

Be first in the know for all Clean Break's news by signing up to our newsletter via our website, or follow us on our social media channels:

Twitter: @CleanBrk
Facebook: /cleanbreak
Instagram: @CleanBrk

CLEAN BREAK STAFF

Erin Gavaghan	Executive Director
Anna Herrmann	Joint Artistic Director
Róisín McBrinn	Joint Artistic Director
Lillian Ashford	Senior Development Manager
Caroline Boss	Marketing Coordinator
Stephanie Cartwright	Philanthropy Manager
Katie Edwards	Studios Administrator
Maya Ellis	Executive Assistant
Mimi Findlay	Producer
Gillian Greer	Creative Associate
Alison Hargreaves	Producer
Ashleigh-Rose Harman	Digital Coordinator
Khaz Khan	Head of Operations
Laura Mallows	Head of Finance & Business
Lorraine Maher	Participation Manager
Selina Mayer	Finance & Data Manager
Samantha McNeil	Volunteer Co-ordinator
Linda Morgans	Cleaner
Sally Muckley	Head of Development & Communications
Jacqueline Stewart	Head of Participation
Katherine Sturt-Scobie	Receptionist
Demi Wilson-Smith	Development and Members Assistant
Dezh Zhelyazkova	Assistant Producer

Clean Break would like to acknowledge the generosity of all its funders and supporters. In particular, Arts Council England, Esmée Fairbairn Foundation and The Backstage Trust for their support of *Inside Bitch*.

Clean Break
2 Patshull Road
London
NW5 2LB

020 7482 8600
general@cleanbreak.org.uk
www.cleanbreak.org.uk

Registered company number 2690758
Registered charity number 1017560

Supported using public funding by
ARTS COUNCIL ENGLAND
LOTTERY FUNDED

THE ROYAL COURT THEATRE

The Royal Court Theatre is the writers' theatre. It is a leading force in world theatre for energetically cultivating writers – undiscovered, emerging and established.

Through the writers, the Royal Court is at the forefront of creating restless, alert, provocative theatre about now. We open our doors to the unheard voices and free thinkers that, through their writing, change our way of seeing.

Over 120,000 people visit the Royal Court in Sloane Square, London, each year and many thousands more see our work elsewhere through transfers to the West End and New York, UK and international tours, digital platforms, our residencies across London, and our site-specific work. Through all our work we strive to inspire audiences and influence future writers with radical thinking and provocative discussion.

The Royal Court's extensive development activity encompasses a diverse range of writers and artists and includes an ongoing programme of writers' attachments, readings, workshops and playwriting groups. Twenty years of the International Department's pioneering work around the world means the Royal Court has relationships with writers on every continent.

Within the past sixty years, John Osborne, Samuel Beckett, Arnold Wesker, Ann Jellicoe, Howard Brenton and David Hare have started their careers at the Court. Many others including Caryl Churchill, Athol Fugard, Mark Ravenhill, Simon Stephens, debbie tucker green, Sarah Kane – and, more recently, Lucy Kirkwood, Nick Payne, Penelope Skinner and Alistair McDowall – have followed.

The Royal Court has produced many iconic plays from Lucy Kirkwood's **The Children** to Jez Butterworth's **Jerusalem** and Martin McDonagh's **Hangmen**.

Royal Court plays from every decade are now performed on stage and taught in classrooms and universities across the globe.

It is because of this commitment to the writer that we believe there is no more important theatre in the world than the Royal Court.

Supported using public funding by
ARTS COUNCIL ENGLAND

ROYAL COURT SUPPORTERS

The Royal Court is a registered charity and not-for-profit company. We need to raise £1.5 million every year in addition to our core grant from the Arts Council and our ticket income to achieve what we do.

We have significant and longstanding relationships with many generous organisations and individuals who provide vital support. Royal Court supporters enable us to remain the writers' theatre, find stories from everywhere and create theatre for everyone.

We can't do it without you.

PUBLIC FUNDING

Arts Council England, London
British Council

TRUSTS & FOUNDATIONS

The Backstage Trust
The Bryan Adams Charitable Trust
The Austin & Hope Pilkington Trust
The Boshier-Hinton Foundation
Martin Bowley Charitable Trust
The Chapman Charitable Trust
Gerald Chapman Fund
CHK Charities
The City Bridge Trust
The Cleopatra Trust
The Clifford Chance Foundation
Cockayne - Grants for the Arts
The Ernest Cook Trust
The Nöel Coward Foundation
Cowley Charitable Trust
The Eranda Rothschild Foundation
Lady Antonia Fraser for The Pinter Commission
Genesis Foundation
The Golden Bottle Trust
The Haberdashers' Company
The Paul Hamlyn Foundation
Roderick & Elizabeth Jack
Jerwood Arts
The Leche Trust
The Andrew Lloyd Webber Foundation
The London Community Foundation
John Lyon's Charity
Clare McIntyre's Bursary
Old Possum's Practical Trust
The Andrew W. Mellon Foundation
The David & Elaine Potter Foundation
The Richard Radcliffe Charitable Trust
Rose Foundation
Royal Victoria Hall Foundation
The Sackler Trust
The Sobell Foundation
Span Trust
John Thaw Foundation
Unity Theatre Trust
The Wellcome Trust
The Garfield Weston Foundation

CORPORATE SPONSORS

Aqua Financial Solutions Ltd
Cadogan
Colbert
Edwardian Hotels, London
Fever-Tree
Gedye & Sons
Greene King
Kirkland & Ellis International LLP
Kudos
MAC

CORPORATE MEMBERS

Gold
Weil, Gotshal & Manges LLP

Silver
Auerbach & Steele Opticians
Bloomberg
Cream
Kekst CNC
Left Bank Pictures
Love My Human
PATRIZIA
Royal Bank of Canada - Global Asset Management
Tetragon Financial Group

For more information or to become a foundation or business supporter contact: support@royalcourttheatre. com/020 7565 5064.

INSIDE BITCH

Conceived by Stacey Gregg and Deborah Pearson

Devised with Lucy Edkins, Jennifer Joseph,
TerriAnn Oudjar and Jade Small

OBERON BOOKS
LONDON

WWW.OBERONBOOKS.COM

First published in 2019 by Oberon Books Ltd
521 Caledonian Road, London N7 9RH
Tel: +44 (0) 20 7607 3637 / Fax: +44 (0) 20 7607 3629
e-mail: info@oberonbooks.com
www.oberonbooks.com

PB ISBN: 9781786827470
E ISBN: 9781786827418

Cover photo credit: Niall McDiarmid
Book design by Konstantinos Vasdekis

Printed and bound by 4EDGE Limited, Hockley, Essex, UK.
eBook conversion by Lapiz Digital Services, India.

10 9 8 7 6 5 4 3 2 1

The Project.

WHAT WE TALK ABOUT WHEN WE TALK ABOUT PRISON

The idea of this project is to explore and challenge public perceptions of prison and women in prison.

To do this, playwright Stacey Gregg and Live Artist Deborah Pearson would like to work with Clean Break graduates with experience of prison. We plan to look at the stories we are told through TV, film and the news that may or may not represent a realistic experience of being in prison.

We will look at popular perceptions of prison through culture and the media. We will then discuss and break down these ideas, and devise together fun, truthful and challenging ways to encourage an audience to think twice about the stories they are told about women in prison.

The process will be agreed with the team of performer/collaborators, and Deborah and Stacey will be in the room and on the floor as much as our Clean Break grads. Together we will find the best way to explore our subject with an audience.

On March 29th we will be meeting Clean Break grads for a chat. This is simply to find a way to put together a group that we think will work well together and bring a variety of experiences to the group. No one will be expected to contribute personal information that they are uncomfortable with.

After this, there will be a few days workshop in June to get to know one another and spark material. Later in the summer there will be a longer process to create the first showing of our project.

Following feedback Deborah and Stacey will redraft and finalise the show for Autumn 2016.

There is no need to prepare for the meeting, other than to perhaps think about the gap between your experience of prison and what other people may have got wrong or right about it.

We look forward to meeting you!

Deborah and Stacey

Artists' Notes.

Lucy Edkins

Having had an intermittent connection with Clean Break going back as far as 1994 – variously as a workshop participant, performer, teacher, stage manager (also here at the Court) and now this time as a professional actor – it's nice to be involved in this production charting Clean Break's new direction, which returns to placing Clean Break Members on an equal playing field. The process has been open and collaborative, and we're lucky to be part of a great company, where everyone's voice is heard.

It's been an interesting journey during the workshop and rehearsal process to see how a moment from our past can be shaped and hyped and exploded until a new character emerges out of the pieces...

You know that moment when your voice goes really low and you can barely get the words out, they come out all stiff but you keep saying them even though your mood is dropping like a stone into a deep chasm.. and it could be words or just a deep low moan that carries on coz you don't have the words the language to tell them what happened. What happened to you. In there. Out there. Before.

Stacey Gregg

Chronology is a bit tidy to me, so I'll jump in at a point of conflict. Conflict is good, right?

I'm quitting theatre again. It's become a bit of a running joke among my friends that I regularly denounce "theatre" and retire. Believe me, I've been trying, but I just can't quit you, theatre.

A few years ago, I was closing up all on-going commitments to theatre. I've always had an uneasy relationship with theatre. I'm not from an artsy background. I'm from a very working class background. Theatre wasn't a thing. I don't know why I was drawn to it, apart from the fact it sounded so romantic. My first intellectual infatuation was with conceptual art and countercultural European theatre texts I'd never seen and probably never will. So my slow realization after moving to London that much theatre is pretty establishment and conservative was a bit of a disappointment. It took me a while to work this out.

Before Clean Break I had done outreach work unrelated to the arts at HMP Holloway. It was some of the hardest work I've ever done with very vulnerable women. Some time later I began a residency with Clean Break in a much more positive and creative role, interacting through prison residencies and working with Clean Break Members in Kentish Town. I'd been commissioned as part of this. But now in this funk of disillusionment I only knew one thing: if I was to create a piece of work for Clean Break it would be examining the representation of women in prison through this very machinery: "theatre" itself. And ideally it would come as directly from the voices of the women as possible. If I was to make theatre it would be anti-theatre, and by that I don't mean simply in opposition to, but more in defiance of the conventions we've become conditioned to accept and valorize and commodify over others.

So I recruited Deborah Pearson, fellow conceptualist, to collaborate on this project to see what might happen.

I knew that there is a kind of impossibility at the heart of any such project, and that in order to make anything we first have to embrace failure. That's lucky, 'cos I like failure. Then, there is the impossibility of trying to represent "reality." The more we *pretend* theatre is "reality," the further away from messy, complex reality we seem to get. I had recently started to recognize this impulse had threaded its way through everything I'd made. My writers voice is compulsively disruptive, fourth wall poking, dissonant, questioning. I'm suspicious of harmonious, tidy voices that tell us what to think. It feels oppressive. And the merry-go-round capitalist imperative that fuels much "theatre" makes me wanna boke.

So, we find ourselves in a workshop with our company. And possibilities emerge. The women are wary of work that represents them as victims, as *issues*, as powerless or without agency. They resent workshops where they are mined for material. And they are funny. We find ourselves laughing our asses of. Catharsis. Tragedy.

We ran a session at Clean Break early on with prison officers from Holloway, shortly after it had been announced, out of the blue, that Holloway would close and be sold as real estate, dispersing both residents and staff outside of London with little notice.

The officers were still reeling; eager to be heard, serious, dedicated. A self-selecting group, sure, just like our company, but nonetheless a sobering insight into how low morale and anxiety seemed an undercurrent of every discussion of the system.

So Deborah and I regroup and refine. Humour is disruptive. And allows the edges of seriousness to be felt all the more keenly. A desire for realness alongside the humour is expressed by the women; our company instinctively know the difference between a feeling of realness versus an attempt to render realism.

It's useful to recognise that no show can be all things to all people. There are so many ways to tackle the criminal justice system or the experience of women in prison, it would be paralyzing to bear the burden of all the urgent conversations that need to be had. We aren't here to lecture. We aren't here to critique these TV prison shows *per se*, but to reflect on how reality is mediated through the entertainment industry, how fiction may come to stand in for reality in the absence of other means of representation. One thing seemed obvious, which is that the actual lives of women in prison are largely invisible. The general public know very little about such worlds apart from what makes it on to TV, or our stages, or our sensational press.

And I have been in many TV writers rooms. I know what I'm talking about here. I know intimately all the corners and limitations and shit-shows of representation in TV and whose voice gets heard and how it can feel when the tectonic plates occasionally shift and a story gets told authentically and how seeing oneself represented in an authentic way can make you feel like you didn't exist before but maybe now you do a little bit.

And so on we went. We generated and amassed tonnes of material through several workshops and Deborah and I slowly begin to order chunks, lightly editing into a shape in consultation with our company. The shape is broadly this: what do shows about women in prison in popular culture look like? What would one made by women who have been in prison look like? I'm not interested in theatre that tells us what to think. The opportunity to point at things and make space for us to think *harder* for ourselves or question the complacently unquestioned is vastly more radical.

It's worth addressing the persistent self-doubt that accompanies making such work: what are the ethical implications, who is it for, how can we resist the inevitable pressure to make something simplistic or "successful" or narratively conventional? Those questions will never entirely be resolved. Making this kind of work exists in live conversation with the historical and cultural particular. We can only make the best and most sensitive and responsible and cheeky work that we can.

And I have only gratitude to everyone who poured their goodwill and energy and patience into this project and most of all to the four women of our company who speak their truth fearlessly and vulnerably and share their grace and resilience every show.

One day while pondering the tone of the piece, I was re-listening to our recordings and discovered what would become the final moment of the show. We're all laughing hard at something when Deborah asks the group "Can you remember a time you really laughed when you were in prison?" The room falls quiet, for an unbearably raw, searching length of time. The pause seems to go on forever. A gear shifts in the cosmos. I suspect it's the quietest our group have ever been. Eventually as one voice they break the silence with dissonance; no, not really.

TerriAnn Oudjar

I didn't really understand the process at the beginning, I just went along with it. They asked me would you like to give some information, I said "yeah, ok, how much you paying me?" I didn't quite understand where it would go. I don't think a lot of people did.

So as it opened up, we've opened up, which has been quite good because I've accepted each step as it comes along. To be at The Royal Court, it hasn't sunk in. I really like the company. I think we work really well together, being really open. I feel like no one's in charge, I've liked that. And I think for me, I haven't felt shut down at all. I'm quite opinionated and I've been allowed to be myself. So I've found the more that's given to me, the more it makes me be myself, because I'll always be myself but sometimes I have to fight for that. And I haven't had to fight. I haven't had to fight,

I've just been allowed to be, because part of me will not change and that might sound arrogant but for me, its because I've spent so many years not knowing who I was and I've done a hell of a lot of work on myself to know myself, the therapy, the ins and outs, the struggles, the trauma, so I've spent thousands of hours trying to analyse, and trying to get to a place of acceptance. This is me. Why am I going to be any different and pretend to be anybody else? So with this process, I've been allowed to be that and it makes my work freer.

I've done lots of work with Clean Break before, and there is a part of me where I find it tiresome, you know: "let's look at another issue," "oh my god its devastating" etc . So with doing *Inside Bitch*, do you want to judge me just because I've been to prison? So you've got this outlook on me? Or if I told you nothing about me at all, without the Clean Break badge, how would you see me? And how does that make me any different? So maybe doing this piece, we might not be able to change that, but we might question your thinking.

Deborah Pearson

I was recently in an interview with two of our cast members when the interviewer (who had seen some of my work in the past) asked the million dollar question, "Most of your work to date has been about you... How did that impact this process?"

It's a tricky question, one that I think a lot of my colleagues who I first met at Forest Fringe and who have come up through contemporary performance also dread. There are so many answers I want to give – among those are:

"Actually I've made at least five shows at this point that I not only wasn't in but where I wasn't a character, a factor, or even a thought in the audience's mind. They were just too expensive to tour and mostly haven't been on in London so you haven't seen them."

Or

"As a woman I resent the implication that if I mention myself in my work the piece is about me. It's the same old thing of men as 'monologuists' and women as 'one woman shows.' When a woman is involved the gender somehow even has to appear in the name – like a warning."

Or

"Just because I've used material from my own life in a performance does not, by any stretch of the imagination, mean that the show is "about me." Please can we all agree to scrap the term "autobiographical theatre" for just this reason. My "autobiographical" shows have all used my presence on stage because they needed to for the concept, etc. etc, also aaaargh!"

But of course I keep these secret responses to myself. Because here I've gone making my artist's note for *Inside Bitch* all about me.

The bigger truth behind all these thoughts is that one of the reasons I've made work that uses my own life as material (aside from the obvious financial constraints around scale that many freelancers work with) is that the ethics of that transaction feel mostly clear. I've found myself changing people's names in my work over the years, asking permission more than I used to when old shows are remounted (but if I'm honest I can still be selective about that too), but as the human on stage holding the story, I know what is at stake for me, and how my relationship to "the truth" can and will change. I know that it will be up to me to deal with it psychologically if someone in the audience is falling asleep while I talk about something that matters hugely to me not only as a performer but as a person. (Word to the wise, avoid performing a show that's 90 minutes long at 11am at the Edinburgh Festival.) Using your own memories on stage is hard work. It's easier for me to parse the difficulty of that work if the memories and the vulnerability are mine and I'm the person who has to perform them and stand behind them on stage.

But I also know how empowering it can feel to stand on stage not in character, but as yourself. I know how exposing that can feel but I think that the empowering part makes the exposing part worthwhile. And through the sharings we've done to this point, I've seen that ring true for our company again and again. **This is not autobiographical theatre.** I'm putting that in bold just in case it wasn't clear. But this is theatre that has a lot of real life in it. The games the company play on stage are real. The jokes they make are theirs. Their sense of humour, their cheeky grins, their buoyant energy as a company is real, and kinetic, and has been thrilling to Stacey and I since the very first workshop. But oddly, I would argue that the most "unreal" part of the show might be where the women appear to tell their own stories – where they re-create their monologues, verbatim, from a story about prison they told us two years ago. Because in this section they are acting themselves in the past, and that self was not the same self who answers questions live on stage or who tries to win a card game or who deftly moves tables around.

If there's anything I learned from work that I appear in, it's that the "self" is not a static thing. If you record it and try to recreate it that will be more apparent than ever. The "self" is a process, and all recordings do is serve to surprise us about who we were and how much we're always changing.

We went around in a circle in one of our rehearsals asking the women what the most important question of the show was for them. TerriAnn asked "Can a Leopard Change Their Spots?" It's an important question for the women, because as TerriAnn reminded us, even if you move on as a person, a criminal record becomes a fact of existence.

My answer to TerriAnn's question would be that the Leopard's spots were never spots to begin with, they were and are a kaleidoscope moving in very slow motion. Just as "autobiographical performance" is an inadequate term because the performer is not a story to be told, but a shifting entity on stage, I hope that this company feels empowered by their own resilience, their own change. They could never really make something that's "about them" – none of us could. But they can *be* themselves on stage and we can fall in love with those real people. And as an audience we can better understand just how insufficient it really is to view anyone through the prism of their past.

The Storyboard.

Beat Sheet.

- SHAWSHANK

- Pre-production: LOCKED UP

- Orange is the New Black: Prison Officer Transcript (list)

- Card Game 1: Material for a Show

- Verbatim Monologues

- Costumes

- Card Game 2: Production Meeting – Focus Group

- P.I.C Trumps

- Setting: Tour of *Inside Bitch*

- Pitch and Trailer

- Red Carpet and "Behind the Scenes" Featurette

- Merch, Reviews, Feedback

- Dance

Shawshank

1.

*JADE steps forward, out of the "picture" from behind
the curtain, and puts on the record player:*

"Marriage of Figaro" plays at top volume.

*The others pause in their jobs. Gaze upward,
appreciatively. Or we imagine they do from what we
can see of them behind the curtain.*

The music swells.

*JEN appears and approaches the sound booth. She enters
it and enacts the following in an American accent as
the others return to their tasks variously:*

> Jen (V.O.)
> I have no idea to this day what
> them two Italian ladies were
> singin' about. Truth is, I don't
> want to know. Some things are best
> left unsaid. I like to think they
> were singin' about something so
> beautiful it can't be expressed in
> words, and makes your heart ache
> because of it.

Beat.

> I tell you, those voices soared.
> Higher and farther than anybody in
> a gray place dares to dream. It was
> like some beautiful bird flapped
> into our drab little cage and made
> these walls dissolve away...and for
> the briefest of moments — every
> last man at Shawshank felt free.

The music stops abruptly.
The others begin walking behind the curtain.
JEN and JADE hurry back to their job and join them.

LOCKED UP
(Gathering Material)

2.

They circle.
They line up behind the curtain.
They discover the curtain.
They peer through the curtain at us, the audience.
A clip begins to play behind the audience

The performers open the curtain a small amount.
They are watching something on a screen.
We cannot see what it is.
They collectively replicate the actions from the clip.
One at a time they may produce a clipboard, and begin to observe
details about the clip in one word sentences, in facts, such as:

Tray.

Gray walls.

Yellow jacket.

White teeth.

Plastic box.

Curly hair.

Eyeballs.

It is as though they are alien scientists.
The clip finishes with a collective beat.

They turn and one of them opens the curtain on the back wall,
something like the kind of traditional curtain you would see in a
cinema, now revealing a screen upon which the clip plays again
with volume, so that we can see it. It is a clip from Spanish TV
series LOCKED UP. The dialogue is in Spanish.

The company watch with us and reaffirm their initial observations,
almost like playing bingo.

Once it has finished, they all look at us.

Clear? Good. On we go.

Orange

Is

the

New

Black

Rant

(list)

3.

One of our company explains that as part of the research for this Project we screened "Orange is the New Black" for prison staff:

Hello everyone.

It's nice to see you all here at the Royal Court.

OK so we did a lot of research.

As part of the research, Deborah and Stacey screened a prison show called "Orange is the New Black" for a bunch of prisoner officers.

They recorded it, and this is the **transcript** of what one male officer had to say. Lucy?

LUCY takes the mic and reads from a clipboard. At some point her tone becomes more authoritative, and by the end rather whiney.

[Excerpt] "Rubbish. And anyone who sees this yeah actually — just carry on, 'cos the quicker we get through this — there's too much in that that was wrong to make it even worth mentioning. I mean you have hierarchies in prison, you have bullying that goes on you have intimidation, harassment that goes on in prison, no way on this Earth would prison staff be as totally and utterly indifferent to what goes on, as they are in that programme. And I know it's about TV, and everyone is made out to be worse than they are 'cos, that's where you get the ratings."

LUCY has really cranked up!

"Those people — none of those people there would be in the job. None of them would be in the job because that is atrocious. No prison would be run that badly. Even our private jails here will not be run that badly. It would never happen. That as 40-odd minutes of my life that I'm never ever gonna get back!!!"

She slams down the clipboard. Wow.

As if to diffuse the atmosphere, JADE has occupied the sound booth and calmly and swiftly relays the following list:

As she speaks the others drift downstage, encircling LUCY and nodding or audibly agreeing with each observation that rings true.

[**Note.** *This list was compiled from workshop material created by the company in response to the question: What do you associate with ideas of prison?*]

Bullying.

Pretty Girl.

Lesbians.

Drugs.

Horrible People.

Horrible Food.

Tracksuits.

Trading.

No TV.

Better than I thought.

Guilty.

Basic, Standard, Enhanced

Tattoo.

Bag in at visits.

Women raping women.

Holiday camp.

Inmate having an affair.

Prisoner beat up in shower.

Phone in cake.

Butch prison dyke running wing.

Rats and Cockroaches.

Days like roman numerals.

Bread and water diet.

Passing drugs on visits.

Escaping prison.

Pussy sucking.

Fighting over chicks.

Swallowing and shitting things out.

Spitting in food.

Drugs.

Decrutching.

Suicide.

Peter Thief — Stealing from each other's cell.

Swooping — Picking up cigarette butts

Depression and mental health.

Knickers on radiators.

Card Game 1

Ingredients from shows
about women in prison

4.

Now all of the performers are around the table, and have set up a card game. Maybe they wear visors and hold cigars. Someone interrupts JADE *and beckons her over.* JADE *joins them as they launch into a familiar, rowdy card game which is built using quotes from TV shows about women in prison.*[1]

It is competitive, it is real, and they each really really want to win.

It may sound something like this:

"I'm heterosexual."

"Oh it makes me come like a werewolf."

"Underwear."

"You step out of line, there will be consequences."

"This is my prison."

"You've got a phone, use it."

"Don't make your bed!"

"I'm just existing."

"I'm only here because of a misunderstanding."

"Sorry about your dildo, boo."

[1] See Appendix for how to play the game.

By now there is haze and backlighting and ash trays making the whole thing feel quite movie-like and iconic.

As they're dealing the second round, discussing how to "win" the game –

JEN: *(Pointedly.)* It all depends what cards you're dealt in life.

The others all turn and give the audience a **very** knowing, wry look: like, lol.

ROUND TWO

*The game grows heated and somehow even more competitive, more **dramatic**. Bigger and faster. They yell the lines each other.*

Until the point where the game explodes, the cards thrown chaotically around.

CRYSTAL the stage manager appears and sweeps up the cards. The others acknowledge her warmly.

Before the dust can settle, JADE addresses the others.

The following, as honest and unaffected as possible.

VERBATIM
Monologues.

5.

Note. these monologues are transcripts from workshops created by the company. They should be ordinary and untheatrical. House lights may be used. The performer may improvise a little in order to maintain the authenticity of the moment.

JADE: Alright here's mine.

Basically I was explaining I had one – well only one sort of big argument in there because ehm

really I had to defend myself, it was more like I don't really wanna but I'm not gonna allow you to do this to me, so that it happens then I'm gonna end up to be bullied.
So when I had this argument with this girl – who was very dramatic and quite funny really 'cos she was running upstairs and I was kickin her down, d'ya know what I mean

I was like that – BOOM – down!

She was comin' – so as far as I'm concerned if you're comin', then obviously that's what you want.

So I'm kicking her down – but that's not the point, the point,

the bit for me was,
the bit for me was,

the next day when I've come out of my cell for breakfast and you know when you look they go "oh look, on telly they've earned their way to the front of the queue", well they've only said that to me, "come to the front of the queue" I was like no, I'll wait in my space... "no no no come to the front of the queue" but I didn't I stayed in my space. But that reminds me of telly, you know like, it's real.

Because you don't. You think that's not really real, obviously you don't argue your way to the front of the queue, but you actually do.
Well you did do there.
But I decided to not go to the front of the queue because

47

she just annoyed me at the time, I wasn't really like that you know, then that came out and they thought I was, aggressive,

cause I stood up for myself the night before

The others are scribbling notes, sticking them up on the whiteboard. They start to discuss JADE's story. How can they use it for their TV show?

Their discussion is interspersed with technical terms used in TV development such as: "jumping the shark" or "nice third act turning point" or "good conflict."

JEN insists that they create a character named Queenie, based off of JADE. Somebody says, "Queenie don't let nobody mess with her." JADE reluctantly agrees to the creation of this fictional character who is really very different to the source material.

They decide that JADE's story makes a great inciting incident. The show is on its way.

TERRIANN: Mine's a little bit funny.

Right, so I'm comin' into jail, I was smacked out, cracked out and wacked out, I'm about seven stone, six and half, seven stone right?

So I'm comin' off the drugs I'm like OK a bit of a nutter,

I got this time to slow down and I think right, I'm gonna go to the gym.

so when you go to prison they don't teach you how to live, what to do, so you've just gotta think, right, fuckin' hell, I'm gonna go to the gym!

But before you've got there you've been eating loadsa rice, you've been eating loadsa potato,
you've just been eating loadsa nothing,
so you've gone from 6 and half stone to 12 stone in a week,

boom!

I'm goin' down the gym. You don't know how to work out. You're such a lunatic! So you go I'm goin' down the gym! Du-doom du-doom du dud dud *(Mimes exercising.)*

so the next minute you're just like pumped up! You're pumped up 'cos you don't know how to do it!

So as time went on I'm walking back down the landing coming back from gym

'cos I got obsessed with the gym

and the girls would hide behind the doors and as I come along every time I made a step they go "Boom. Boom. Boom. Boom."

So hence from that I got the nickname Pitbull

and they go here comes Pitbull! And you know the maddest thing you'd do it every time you went to jail.

More discussion from the women about how to use this story in their TV show. It's got a nickname! It's got a catchphrase! The women nearly chant the catchphrase with each other with relish – OY, here comes Pitbull! They talk about how the scene provides comic relief. They find a place to put it in the narrative arc of the show. Two characters, one catchphrase, they're making progress. So who's next?

LUCY: Okay so for mine there's this girl called Beadie who's in the next cell, she's ah, a self-proclaimed thief you know, young black girl, she's lovely to come and –

and then next cell to her there's this girl who's very pretty and ehm is in for a really nasty crime, and she's got these two very pretty girls who are her kind of posse, kind of thing.

And it's a strange gang 'cos they're just three very pretty girls, but she's em, I can't remember what she did to Beadie but everyone that I sort of hung out with was I guess was tryna help Beadie get back at her. And I wasn't you know part of this big plan but I was kind of pulled in.

Everyone went into the TV room and they were in there, the pretty girls were in there, and ah I and Karina, who's the cheeky one on the wing, is chattin to me and she got me to put on my James Brown tape and its Sex Machine,

and so I was kinda chattin away to her, doin the splits,

and she was goin' "yeah yeah!"

and we were carryin on like that – meanwhile in there the lights are off and Beadie's attacked this girl with a broken bit of a Nescafe glass,
and I've been a sort of...

decoy.

I didn't realise I was the decoy. But I didn't – I didn't like the girl – 'cos what I did for everybody, I did portraits for cigarettes, portraits for tabacco. So she give me a picture of her...um um her brother and it came out all wrong

I couldn't get it!

The women really like this story. It's funny, it's violent. There's some talk about LUCY's character name – should it be... The Decoy? Nah. She didn't know she was a decoy. How about... The Artist? LUCY loves this nickname. She's got an idea... How about we feature a scene with the artist's paintbrush? But the others get confused... A paintbrush? What's dramatic about a paintbrush? They need viewers. Focus on the violence. Maybe get in some drugs. LUCY seems agreeable and the conversation moves on.

There may be some discussion about the need for "sexy crime." But what the women reveal is that in reality they only ever knew women in prison for nicking coffee from Lidl, or not paying their poll tax, or their kid playing truant. No "sexy" violent crime. In

fact, most women are in prison for mental health reasons or because they were victims in the first place.

Nonetheless, the Nescafe's story appeals. It goes up on the board – a kind of violent climax.

So far, JADE's and TERRIANN's moments have been quite ordinary stories, about queuing for lunch or the gym. LUCY's was ordinary but there was some violence.

Here, the tone shifts. JEN's moment is very challenging. She may enter the soundbooth in order to share it with us.

JEN: Em, I mean, my – uh my – my moments like they, 'cos I got kids, I got three children so basically a lot around it and.

So f- in the first instance, putting my kids, ah getting stopped at the airport and your kids being there was -, that moment in itself was sort of like

"can you come with us miss?" "yeah alright, but do me a favour, don't let my kids see." That's your first reaction. So you're more – you're more or less giving yourself up, d'you know what I mean, you know yourself like. So that was traumatic.

They put me in another room, took me in another room, and went through my cases and that, and – no no they didn't actually 'cos they put them in a room, I said is it alright if I call my husband to come and get them, you know what I mean, so they let me do all of that, thinking back in hindsight I shoulda said um "yeah! take this, and take this case and take – " you know what I mean? *[Laughs.]* And I probably woulda got away with it a bit, you know what I mean, but you're not thinking that 'cos it's just about the kids isn't it so...

my husband came, everyone's crying, and so then that's bad enough, so now I'm nicked and I'm inside and they've gotta go through the the undignified way of getting searched and and all of that and they're adults – they're big people now – but they were, my son was 10.

And uh they'd been comin' on the visits I mean like so much so *every single day* even when I was *sentenced*, 'cos everyone knew even in the prison, everyone was used to them, screws were really nice to them, it was "Jen, your kids are here" you know what I mean? it was a nice -. And I think it was on the em, maybe the fourth, fifth, maybe sixth visit, they come in and

I never, ever ever in my whole life thought that I would even *consider* something that went through my head –

you know and they sort of come in they're sitting down and you're already at the point where I don't – I *do* wanna hear what's going on in your lives, but I can't do nothing about it d'ya know what I mean? So I thought

my kids would be quite strong and you know I was very proud of them. And they came on one visit and like my daughter said to me like you know like "the neighbours know" and I said "how do the neighbours know?" 'cos I'm a very private person, and I said – and she said uh, mum they know and I just wanted you to know they know 'cos I know you was trying to – and I said but how do they know? What are you lot going around telling the neighbours for that I'm in jail for importation you know what I'm saying?

and she said mum we didn't tell anyone and I said well how do they know then, you know what I mean? And she said my em, my son, who you know is just my pride and joy, he's so precious to me... 'cos I had an ectopic before him and an ectopic after him do you know what I mean? So I was just blessed – she said to me just don't get angry but I'm just gonna tell ya I said I'm not gonna get angry with you lot you know at a time like now and she said uh ...

He went out to play and uh

Perhaps "long pause" is projected. JEN takes a moment.

and then this play area, the kids they play with they – they come out and they said to him "what's the matter" 'cos he was crying...

and then they said to him what's the matter and he said "aw, my mum's in jail."

And I thought – my first thought was – after I got over it – well why didn't you do that inside with your sisters like?

And then it dawned on me that you know actually, they're not really dealing with it are they do you know what I mean?

And at that moment I thought I really wanna tell my kids, don't come back and see me. Let me just get my nut down, do it, and I can come home.

Sorry

Perhaps the word "Upset" is now projected. JEN pauses again for a moment before continuing.

But you can't can you? You can't look at your kids and say don't come and see me 'cos I can't handle it, because they can't handle it...

I will never to this blessed day forgive myself for putting my children through that experience, even though they've said to me, we forgive you mum, that's that's that's the least – we love you to the bone, so anything you do can never hurt or upset us 'cos you're only doing it for us, do you know what I mean?

Pause.

TERRIANN: I think that we can all agree that's the emotional climax of the show.

But there is an atmosphere following JEN's monologue.
Allow the audience to feel it.
This is uncomfortable, right?

COSTUMES

6.

Music interrupts the moment.

A rack emerges of personalised jumpsuits, in our show lime green.

The women use this as a way to transition out of the heavy moment. They rearrange the tables like a craft workshop and get to work personalizing their jumpsuits.

They have their nicknames emblazoned on the back of their jumpsuits: "Muvva," "The Artist," "Pitbull," and "Queenie."

The women complete their respective tailored outfits and put them on, in a mockery of a sexy "routine". A reverse striptease. JEN, as ever, is completely pissed off with this development but the others keep including her, encouraging her on.

At the end of the routine –

TERRIANN: A little fact for you, you know women's prisons in the UK don't actually ever have uniforms or jumpsuits?

But we look good right?

A wink.

Now costumed and energized, the women rearrange the tables like a quiz show and gather for:

Card Game 2

Focus Group
(Production Meeting)

7.

Perhaps TERRIANN writes "PRODUCTION MEETING" up on the whiteboard, or the fruitbowl is replenished.

Diagrams of story structure and TV show formula appear on the projection screen.

A card game, using a buzzer/egg timer. The audience are our FOCUS GROUP. We are brainstorming elements for the show, some of which are open to audience participation.

Each QUESTION is picked out of a pile and read aloud with an instruction for how many play, and how long players get.

Among them, for example:

- **To play:** All of us
  Timing: 1 min
  To ask: Name all of the films, plays, TV shows and books about prison that you can.

- **To play:** All cast
  Timing: 1 min
  To ask: List all your qualifications for *Inside Bitch*

- **To play:** 1 Player
  Timing: 1 min
  To ask: Answer the question what do you think of the monologues in the show? Using real stories?

- **To play:** All cast
  Timing: 1 min
  To ask: Talk about diversity in *Inside Bitch*

- **To play:** All of us
  Timing: 1 min
  To ask: Ask everyone to brainstorm names for a porno about women in prison

- **To play:** All cast
  Timing: 1 min
  To ask: Organise the other cast members as an *Inside Bitch* photoshoot and take a pic

- **To play:** All of us
  Timing: 1 min
  To ask: Ask how many soap characters we can name who have been to prison

- **WILD CARD**
  To play: All of us
  Timing: 1 min
  To ask: Ask the audience if anyone has a question they'd like to ask.

- **To play:** All cast
  Timing: 1 min
  To ask: Talk about Stacey and Deborah's process for *Inside Bitch*.

- **To play:** All cast
  Timing: 1 min
  To ask: Talk about Paddington Bear going to prison.

Perhaps the buzzer grows louder and more intrusive, a suggestion that some other power is strangely and suddenly in control.

Perhaps this is where we get a flash of some REAL TITLES and IMAGES of prison movies about women.

The EGG TIMER tells us the game is over after six QUESTIONS.

Now what?

LUCY excitedly floats a new game:

P.I.C TRUMPS

8.

LUCY: Anyone ever played P.I.C Trumps?

JADE: Nah

TERRIANN: Haven't heard of it.

LUCY: It's interesting actually. It's complicated but it's interesting. It could be useful as research.

TERRIANN: We could give it a go.

They rearrange the tables for card playing.

LUCY: Alright I need six cards. "Public", "Media", "Politician", "Warden", "Prisoner", "Guard" – Ah that's actually six and there are only four of us so two of us can do two things, I guess. Alright

(Deals out those cards.)

If you've got the Ace you're the Public, King is media, Queen is Politician, Jack is Warden, 10 is Guard, 9 is Prisoner. So check your card and don't let anyone see it. Now keep your cards and I'm going to deal out the rest of the deck. So it's a bit like "Mafia" combined with "Asshole". Has anyone played those?

(No one has.)

Right okay

(Reading instructions from a huge oversized and overcomplicated card. The others occasionally try to interrupt or ask questions but LUCY just wants to get through this.)

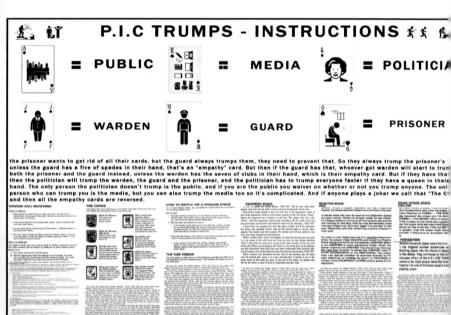

P.I.C TRUMPS - INSTRUCTIONS

= PUBLIC **= MEDIA** **= POLITICIA[N]**

= WARDEN **= GUARD** **= PRISONER**

the prisoner wants to get rid of all their cards, but the guard always trumps them, they need to prevent that. So they always trump the prisoner's unless the guard has a five of spades in their hand, that's an "empathy" card. But then if the guard has that, whoever got warden will start to trum[p] both the prisoner and the guard instead, unless the warden has the seven of clubs in their hand, which is their empathy card. But if they have tha[t] then the politician will trump the warden, the guard and the prisoner, and the politician has to trump everyone faster if they have a queen in their hand. The only person the politician doesn't trump is the public, and if you are the public you waiver on whether or not you trump anyone. The onl[y] person who can trump you is the media, but you can also trump the media too so it's complicated. And if anyone plays a joker we call that "The C[…]" and then all the empathy cards are reversed.

MOVING AND MORPHING

HOW TO BATTLE ON A MISSION SPACE

THE EGG TOWER

EQUIPMENT SPACE

OBJECTIVE SPACE

SNEAK ATTACK SPACE

So the prisoner wants to get rid of all their cards, but the guard always trumps them, they need to prevent that. So they always trump the Prisoner's cards unless the Guard has a five of spades in their hand, that's an "empathy" card. But then if the guard has that, whoever got Warden will start to trump both the Prisoner and the Guard instead, unless the Warden has the seven of clubs in their hand, which is their empathy card. But if they have that, then the Politician will trump the Warden, the Guard and the Prisoner, and the Politician has to trump everyone faster if they have a Queen in their hand. The only person the Politician doesn't trump is the Public, and if you are the Public you waiver on whether or not you trump anyone. The only person who can trump you is the Media, but you can also trump the Media too so it's complicated. And if anyone plays a joker we call that "The Crash" and then all the empathy cards are reversed. Is everyone following?

TERRIANN: No not really.

LUCY: We don't have to play...

LUCY's game is TOO COMPLICATED. The others are bored.

SETTING

9.

Now what?

Ok, what's our precinct for the show? You know, the setting?

What's our prison going to look like?

JADE begins to remember and describe her own personal experience and memory of prison:

Tour of INSIDE BITCH

They get up and JADE begins hosting a fake tour of the prison, mapping it out on top of the playing space in minute detail.

At first the others play visitors on the tour, outsiders with questions and challenges. The following is taken verbatim from a workshop exercise.

JADE: It's a small space. We're just waiting to go across because we need clearance OK? So we're just gonna wait and then we can see where the ladies work. So prepare yourselves. Right so let's go through. Through here is lots and lots of women, loads of them, boisterous. The ceilings are very high. And they'd be over to you like a shot right now. OK so you imagine there's a lot of people who probably want your shoes. OK so let's go along. And there's doors all along here and these all show the workshops, all along.

TERRIANN: Should we talk to them if they approach us?

JADE: Don't forget they're human.

TERRIANN: OK

JEN: What's up there?

JADE: The ceilings are really high. Just to let you know the ceilings are really high. These are all doors to workshops. I used to work in the hairnet store. But out here was probably the most vulnerable I felt because it wasn't really watched enough. And there was this girl called Catherine and she was

such a bully it was unbelievable. But you know in the end,
you'd all be really proud of me, because I said "do you know
what, you can just fuck off bruv!" Because I was just vexed
in the end. But she was really aggressive. I mean she used
to beat up her girlfriend, and like we'd be like obviously we
couldn't help her girlfriend because her girlfriend would go
back out with her.

JEN: Where is she right now? While we're on the tour is she on
the block?

JADE: She will be here somewhere. She's working in one of
these rooms.

TERRIANN: Is she gonna bother us?

JADE: Well if she bothers you...

TERRIANN: We'll beat her up

JADE: (Suddenly stern.) We won't have that, OK?

TERRIANN: Ok.

JADE: And as you come along there's lots and lots of people.
Would you like to go into one of these workshops?

ALL: Yeah yeah!

JADE: Alright ok. So as we enter into one of these workshops
it is literally: table, table, table, table, tables everywhere, and
they're all, there's lots of women all sitting there. They'll all
turn and say hi.

LUCY: Where'd you eat? Like where did those women say that
thing to you about the front of the queue?

JADE: Well if you through here this was my dining hall.

*At this point JADE goes "off script" and begins to improvise,
continuing to describe her dinner hall.*

But now there is dissent as TERRIANN *breaks away and begins her own tour of her own dinner hall while* JADE *carries on.*

TERRIANN: No, no, no that's not how it was for me. It was different. My memory is Holloway...

She continues to tell the audience about her own personal memory.

Eventually LUCY *starts her own tour, no, no, mine was like this.*

And finally, with an "if you can't beat 'em" shrug, JEN *launches into hers, no, no, no mine was like* this.

As ever, they grow bigger and more competitive, overlapping and lost in each of their own subjective rememberings until:

Add soundtrack, The Shawshank "Marriage of Figaro" blasts. At some point we see each of them carrying their trays and food along a queue, but different queues, from different memories. The effect is choreographed, chaotic, impassioned, heightened.

Perhaps light is used to map out their memories.

As the energy peaks they gather and psych each other up as it's time to:

P
I
T
C
H
!

10.

They rearrange themselves.

JADE may be seated on the table and they roll her downstage and strike a pose.

Perhaps they don huge corporate shoulder pads and sit on the table facing us like the front cover of WORKING GIRL .

All the elements we've encountered throughout the show are now poured into their big SELL. It is big and grotesque and tacky and funny. And they know it.

JADE: Okay so I know what you're thinking. You're thinking, "Not another television show about women in prison." Right?

You've seen *Orange Is the New Black*. You've seen *Locked Up*. You've seen *Bad Girls* – the TV show *and* the musical. So what have we got that's different? Well, for one, we've all been to prison. We know what it's like. We know what was funny, we know what was boring, we know what was sad. And we know what mum and dad sitting at home in front of a telly on a Saturday night want to see.

We've got the real shit, and trust me, it's dark as fuck, and it will knock your socks off.

Also, this would be set in the UK, yeah?

And it *won't* star a blonde woman.

TERRIANN: So it opens with Muvva, a strong black woman. She's stood with her two children in a line-up at the airport. She's having all sorts of lovely chat with her beautiful children. When suddenly we hear a voice. It's a guard. He's saying, "Excuse me Miss. Can you step right this way?" Everything goes hazy. Her daughter looks up at her, confused. Her son says, Mummy? She looks down to the case she's gripping by the handle, and we see that her hands are sweating.

And we know that her life is about to change forever.

Each performer really supports the others and cuts in on and tops the previous, upping the ante.

LUCY: Cut to another character. The Artist. A blonde woman, but a bit older, and already settled in the prison. She's sat by the window to the prison with her hand stuck out the window, waiting for something. We hear another woman's voice yelling "Geronimo!" and a sock with a battery in it swings down past the window, as Lucy sticks her hand out. Tied to the bottom of the sock is...

LUCY makes the decision to rebel. She steps away from the others, and finds someone in the audience who she thinks might understand... The others are trying to pull her back, but LUCY is off to the races.

LUCY: ...a paintbrush.

The Artist catches it in her hand and says, "Bullseye." She yells back up, "Thanks Beadie!" and turns to her room. We see there are books in her cell, there are postcards stuck to the wall, and she's sitting in front of an easel, trying to paint a photograph of a girl and her brother. She throws out her old paintbrush and takes her new paintbrush off of the sock and battery.

She starts touching up a sunset behind the painting she has done of the girl and her brother, but then she swears. "This isn't right yet," she says. "It's just not right!"

TERRIANN gets things back on track.

TERRIANN: Cut to Muvva. She's stood in line at the cafeteria. She looks anxiously around the caf. There are frightening characters everywhere.

JEN: In front of her in the line up there's a real trouble maker. She's pushing the other women around. When we see Queen.

Queenie doesn't let anyone mess with her. She turns around to the pushy woman and says, "Fuck off Bruv!" And the woman stops pushing and quietly mumbles, "Excuse me."

Just then, we see the women at the front of the queue. Real nasty but tough types. Think *Mean Girls* but in prison. They turn to Queenie and say, "Hey, you." Queenie seems surprised. "Who me?" And the Mean Girls say, "Yeah. You. Come here. Join us at the front of the queue."

Queenie looks around and briefly makes eye contact with Muvva. Who is new, but she sees it all. She sees Muvva's fear, her confusion, and it reminds her of herself once upon a time. She decides she won't become hardened. She won't invest too hard in this strange place she's found herself.

She says, "Thanks ladies, but I'm alright."

LUCY: Just then, a very built blonde woman comes trundling across the caf and everyone starts yelling

ALL: "Boom. Boom. Boom."

TERRIANN: "Oy!" they yell!

ALL: *(With the relish of a catchphrase!)* "Here Comes Pitbull!"

JADE: So already you can see this prison show is a real patchwork of deeply loveable characters and moments. And that's what sets it apart from the rest.

TERRIANN: Also it's got a brilliant name. We're calling it

ALL: "Inside Bitch."

Now the women melt away as their **TRAILER** *plays: it is bananas and bears no resemblance to the elements they have carefully been building! It contains elements of some of the phrases and monologues we have heard. However we never see our individual company members. Remember they have built the show, rather than "starred" in it.*

RED CARPET and FEATURETTE
(Post-production)

11.

A red carpet awards speech moment.

A live feed that follows JADE *being voxpopped on her way into the Royal Court's launch night. The others become the press pit,*

JADE *is focused on the photographers beyond and doesn't have much time for the press questions.*

"What are you wearing tonight?"

"How do you feel as a white woman taking a part meant for a black woman?"

"What work have you got lined up after this?"

"Did you ever think going to prison would pay off like this?"

The moment ends with JADE *shutting it down with a "no comment!"*

Followed by a brief, earnest awards ceremony acceptance speech, something along the lines of – "Coming through Clean Break I could never have imagined myself standing here on this stage accepting this award for Best New TV Show. But things are changing. You're all so sweet."

Now a "Making Of" Featurette plays, made up of content from the rehearsal room, auditions, "Inside Bitch" on tour. Perhaps at least one serious to camera moment from one of our company, ending on a note of candour about why they're involved in "Inside Bitch."

In this production we had the cast do self tapes, audition as themselves and each other, recite the lyrics to "Chicago" songs. We used green screen to mock up "Inside Bitch" on tour to LA, New York, Paris, Siberia. Also to make the iconic final scene of Thelma and Louise and "You ain't my mother!" from "EastEnders".

MERCH

12.

*Lights up. NOW they reveal their dementedly optimistic range of **merchandise**, everything emblazoned with the INSIDE BITCH brand. Caps, bumbags, lighters, a banana.*

JADE: What are we going to do with all this shit?

The company look uncertain.

TERRIANN: Watch and learn!

They shuffle together, eyeballing each other, then us.

They simultaneously start FLOGGING the merch to the audience. They really sell things. Money changes hands.

REVIEWS

13.

INSIDE BITCH
27 February – 23 March 2019
Royal Court

The company distribute Clean Break **evaluation forms** to the audience, except this is actually aimed at the audience. Maybe they each pick an audience member to fill out the form with.

For eg. How well did we do? Are we feeling ok? Multiple choice: did I concentrate? Mark 1 to 5.[2]

Crystal the stage manager brings out the reviews. They pass around the papers, go off to their separate corners, and all quietly have a read. The odd "oh" or "hmph." Each night one of the company eventually read one review from a changing list. It is, essentially, a warm if verbose and slightly patronising review, drawn from reviews of other shows that deal with similar subject matter.

The group engage once again directly with the audience. Possibly, a discussion about the language used in the press by critics. The emails addressing this between their PR and journalists (using real Inside Bitch correspondence).

Perhaps they remark on the failure or impossibility of Deborah and Stacey's intentions.

In fact, they never wanted to make this show anyway. They never wanted to make a show about prison. You just end up repeating all the same old tropes. There're tonnes of things they'd rather be making shows about!

[2] See Appendix

77

SET TO SELF-DESTRUCT

14.

LUCY *makes her way over to the record player from the start of the show, as the others continue to discuss.*

LUCY *takes out a special record. Puts it on. The others start to react.*

It's the song "Instant Hit" by The Slits. They all begin to move.

There's a joyful unleashing in this strange end of show dance... It's on their own terms.

They strip off the "costumes."

And suddenly the dance collapses back into their jobs from the beginning of the show: unaccompanied, unadorned, real-time, each in their individual reality.

The music has finished.

They pull down the curtain.

They stop, watch us.

Pretty much the realest thing we've seen.

A final recording plays of the women from when they were in workshops for the show:

DEBORAH'S VOICE: "Can you remember a time you laughed really hard when you were in prison?"

A very, very long pause.

A pause so long we think it might be a technical error.

JEN'S VOICE: "You know I can't?"

JADE'S VOICE: "No sorry, I can't. I'm struggling to remember laughing but I can't.."

The recording fades out.

Silence.

Stillness.

Finally, lights down.

END.

End Notes.

Hell Penitentiary
Nightmare in Badham County
Orange Is the New Black
Ilsa the Wicked Warden
Riot in a Women's Prison
Caged Women
Sharkansas Women's Prison
Massacre
Chained Heat 2
Women in Cell Block 7
Women's Prison Massacre
Femmes in Prison
Under Lock and Key
House of Women
Women's Prison Massacre
Uncut!
Escape From a Women's Prison
Prison Heat

Caged Heat!
Fugitive Girls
Chicks in Chains
Prison a go go
Bad Girls
Barbed Wire Dolls
Run Away Girls
Women in Cages
The Big Bird Cage
Caged Seduction
The Smashing Bird
Escape from Hell
Condemned Women
Women in Chains
Bare Behind Bars
Stuck!
The Naked Cage
Dracula in a Women's Prison

Monologues

The monologues were developed from a workshop where we explored the company's memories and thoughts of experience in prison. They were then delivered verbatim in production, apart from identifying or too personal details which were removed.

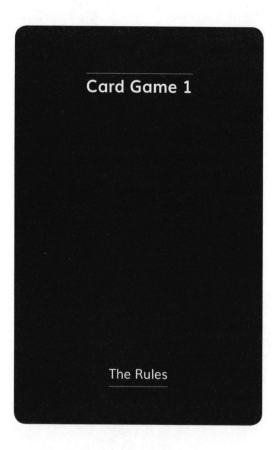

Card Game 1

The Rules

Each of the cards has a different line of dialogue from a prison TV show written on it.

The following are the lines from the rehearsal cards for *Inside Bitch*. These lines were gathered by the company when we watched clips from prison dramas together. The lines on the cards in performance differ.

"Oh it makes me come like a Werewolf" (Whoever gets this card goes first.)

"That's just the cost of doing business."

"I feel stupid for being in here."

"Post! Somebody loves you today."

"I'm just existing."

"You know I drove like three hours to get here."

"That's not drugs."

"They only do it like that to wind us up."

"Sorry about your dildo, boo."

"Fuckin white girl speaks Spanish."

"Don't make your bed."

"I'm expecting a letter from my solicitor."

"I'm only in here because of a misunderstanding."

Around 40 cards are dealt out between the four performers.

The aim of the game is to get rid of all of your cards first, by throwing them into the centre of the table.

In order to get rid of a card you need to say the line of dialogue written on the card, without speaking at the same time as another player or interrupting another player.

The performers are the referees, and the game's rules evolve through them over time.

Loser deals.

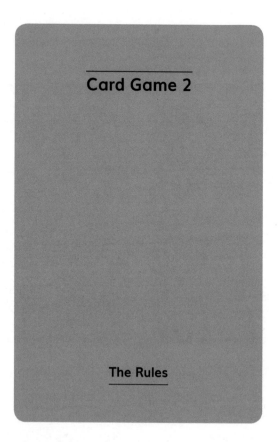

Card Game 2

The Rules

There are around ten cards, five on each of the two tables. Alex Trebek style, the women take turns reading out the instructions written on the back of the card. Almost all of the tasks are timed to one minute. Some of the tasks involve gentle participation from the audience.

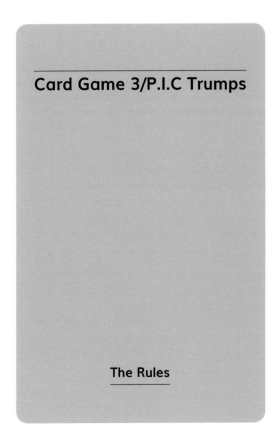

Card Game 3/P.I.C Trumps

The Rules

As far as we know, this game is impossible to play.

Reviews

Excerpts of real reviews repurposed for *Inside Bitch*.

Four real-life ex-prisoners share their stories with us in this powerful, if somewhat unfocused, piece of theatre. Created by Stacey Gregg and Deborah Pearson, *Inside Bitch* brings home the various ways popular culture fetishizes incarcerated women.

They all appear as themselves rather than impersonated by actors in a piece that embraces various performance styles. Any misgivings that this "casting" decision would turn *Inside Bitch* into a freak show for titillated voyeurs are quickly dispelled. It's a great tribute to all concerned that the production generates such a warm atmosphere of trust.

The exceptional sense of emotional immediacy is only enhanced by the clearly spontaneous moments when some had to fumble for their lines or fight to retain their composure at the performance I saw. It is, rightly and responsibly, disarming. I would have liked a strand where these shrewd, witty people talked about whether they have come to think of themselves as, in any way, a self-selecting group.

Part show, part confessional therapy session, it allows four women who have been to prison to tell us the kind of show about prison they would make themselves.

Under the auspices of Clean Break's graduate scheme, speaking out about their own experience makes it impossible to judge the evening as a piece of theatre. Its aims and its impact lie elsewhere.

At numerous points I was reminded of Michael Bennett's 1974 experiment where he gathered a bunch of 'gypsies' together in a room, provided them with awful wine and set the tape rolling, asking them to talk about their life, their experience and real-life troubles.

The cast finally break through the fourth wall that they've been chipping away at throughout the evening and allow the piece to progress from the voyeuristic tendencies to a fully integrated and connected display of truth and intimacy.

The sense of confrontation is low level but palpable, from the language of the show's title, to the audience interaction. It seems somewhat counterintuitive to this critic to use language such as "bitch" in a piece which purports to show us another side of women in prison.

Job Material

Performer 1: Put it in the machine, now the powder, scoop and shake, scoop and shake. Now the liquid. Pick up, tip over put down go back shut the door shut the door, turn it on. Put it in the machine, now the powder, scoop and shake, scoop and shake. Now the liquid. Pick up, tip over put down go back shut the door shut the door, turn it on. / Put it in the machine, now the powder, scoop and shake, scoop and shake. Now the liquid. Pick up, tip over put down go back shut the door shut the door, turn it on. Put it in the machine, now the powder, scoop and shake, scoop and shake. Now the liquid. Pick up, tip over put down go back shut the door shut the door, turn it on. Put it in the machine, now the powder, scoop and shake, scoop and shake. Now the liquid. Pick up, tip over put down go back shut the door shut the door, turn it on.

Performer 2: Taking the bag in, put it down, open close and clothes down clothes out clothes down, wipe the sweat, pick the load up, put it in, powder, scoop sprinkle, liquid, pour down, kick, bum, elbow. Taking the bag in, put it down, open close and clothes down clothes out clothes down, wipe the sweat, pick the load up, put it in, powder, scoop sprinkle, liquid, pour down, kick, bum, elbow. / Taking the bag in, put it down, open close and clothes down clothes out clothes down, wipe the sweat, pick the load up, put it in, powder, scoop sprinkle, liquid, pour down, kick, bum, elbow. Taking the bag in, put it down, open close and clothes down clothes out clothes down, wipe the sweat, pick the load up, put it in, powder, scoop sprinkle, liquid, pour down, kick, bum, elbow.

Performer 3: We're all standing in a line. Ready? We've got the mop, we'll hold the mop there always right so step to the right bring your foot in and mop. Step to the left, and we're gonna swoop almost. We'll do the same again but with a turn. So we turn and repeat the swoop , turn and repeat the same movement. The next bit is, like when you're shaking rubbing your hands together. 1, 2, 3, 4, hold the mop. Now we're gonna wring the mop out but we're gonna bring our bodies down in a robotic kind of movement with the hand. 1, 2, 3, 4, 5, 6, 7, 8 and stop.

Oitnb Prison Staff Session: Transcription

DP Why were you interested in coming onboard with this project?

3 I thought it's a way to sort of advocate, and give, perhaps a balanced view, or an honest view, you compared to what the media puts out there and stuff...

1 I think unfortunately what happens through any drama programme that is on, it's always portrayed that the prisoners are all good and well behaved and the staff are all bad, have affairs and bring in phones and drugs –

SG Is that not what happens?

(Laughter)

1 and unfortunately in the media, in the media anything that's ever reported, certainly with Holloway is anything that's ever happened that's bad, and I don't mean bad as in somebody gets beaten up I mean bad as in a death in custody, or you know something that the Government may suggest, and anything good that happens in prison never gets reported, and that's because no one's interested in good, and that's the same for any huge business or company I'm sure. But it's nice – and that's what I thought about coming here, that if you are writing something that you do get the right terminology and you do see a different side to it. I.e. the staff side and you see the work that's done and the care that's given to women that come into the system...

SG One of the interesting things that came out of being at *** was the Governor there said they can't actually be public about some of the good work they do there because the press will immediately jump on it and be like "oh look swimming lessons for criminals" so there's actually a kind of self-censorship ...

1 You do talk to family and friends and say we do this in prison we do that – they get this? And they're shocked that they get that. What do you expect that they get in prison? How do you think they're treated? 'Cos if we're gonna lock that door and throw away the key you're only gonna put out that person or someone worse, it's very hard to put that across to people who don't know that system that you know, these women need help, they need care, not to go back out into that system. Unfortunately you don't see that in drama, in books...

3 Absolutely, just to follow up on what *** said, I remember when we first went to prison and we do the tour of the prison, I was really shocked to see like the nail salon, the swimming pool, I was like oh my gosh this could be some sort of two star hotel, and then we started working with children and families, it was so crucial, key that these mothers attended perhaps nail bar or hair salon or whatever, because when the children came away and realised you know mum looked good, smelt well, she wasn't dishevelled, it made them feel so relieved, "wow so it's not what I thought" so it was so important they had some sort of therapy, the ability to keep themselves clean, look good you know within reason. So I could see why that was crucial, key to help them cope with the anxiety the stress of losing their children, 'cos it's totally different to have a woman pulled out of a family unit than it is a man. [...] The other things is the design, the factory workshop – how much time have we spent doing that up and you know wonderful things have come out of it and to know now that it's going to close, but I remember when that was on the news and this had been launched, and one of the members of the royal family came to open it or something and people were in uproar! Oh my gosh is this what the government's done they've spent so much money on this – they just got the wrong end of the stick, they didn't understand ...

SG It always strikes me as amazing how misunderstood rehabilitation is ...

2 There's quite a lot of problems within that. Let's be clear. If an individual commits the crime. They deserve the punishment. No issues no problems with that whatsoever. You commit the crime you take the punishment. Rehabilitation is all about assisting that person to get through to the end of it to say OK, you've realised the mistakes you have made, maybe of your own making, may not be, maybe because of your upbringing, maybe because of your lifestyle maybe because of what you were taking, but the end result is to assist that person to see where they're coming from to see where they maybe are going to . And part and parcel of that is the manual workshop, allowing people to go out to work, to understand what it means to have a job, a lot of these people won't have had a job. As a male member of staff in this environment to give these women a positive male role model [...]

The Process.

THELMA & LOUISE

Prison Memoirs on the couch with *Lorraine*

Review.

heres an Insight into a truthful
Perseption of The Criminal Justice
System, the whole, truth and nothing
but The truth, is a heart werenching
funny, and shocking story
about A fantastic woman Called

Jade Small who talks frankly
about her experiences Inside ~~the~~

Prison.

5 ✳ The Daily Mail

A 1000mls of METHADONE
AND A BIKINI

Hold on tight, get ready for a rollercoaster
of highs and lows (litraly).
TerriAnn is a lost teenager who falls apart
after her mum dies, she sets of in search
~~for~~ to find herself, she falls in love, in prison
and out. An adventure to follow with love,
drugs crime, passion, ~~and~~ a moving novel
with hope and laughter.

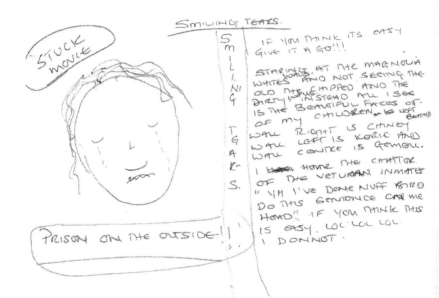

STUCK MOVIE

SMILING TEARS.

S
m
i
l
i
N
G

T
G
A
K.
S.

IF YOU THINK ITS EASY GIVE IT A GO!!!

STARING AT THE MAGNOLIA WHITES/WALLS AND NOT SEEING THE OLD THREADBARE CHIPPED AND THE DIRTY INSTEAD ALL I SEE IS THE BEAUTIFUL FACES OF OF MY CHILDREN LEFT BEHIND WALL RIGHT IS CHINEY WALL LEFT IS KONIK AND WALL CONTRE IS GEMELL. I HEAR THE CHATTER OF THE VETURAN INMATES " YH I'VE DONE NUFF BIRD DO THIS SENTONCE ON ME HEAD". IF YOU THINK THIS IS EASY. LOL LOL LOL. I DONNOT.

PRISON ON THE OUTSIDE!!

99

This is a hand-drawn mock-up of a book cover. The front cover shows the title "The Fall & Rise OF LUCY E." with a figure swinging above water.

Front cover:

The Fall & Rise OF LUCY E.

Spine:

The Fall & Rise of Lucy E   Macmillan paperback

Back cover:

'This rollacoaster ride takes ~~the~~ nomadic childhood through ~~early separation~~ of family break-up, descent into depravity + the slow climb ~~to~~ back to acceptance + self fulfilment

a heartfelt memoir from an ~~emerging~~ which has talent, previously gone unnoticed

~~Jeremy~~ Spalding ~~spectator~~

~~A~~ refreshing sideways look at ~~the~~ underclass and who is or is not accepted ~~that the a~~

7.99

SBN
347011
XIIIV

A letter to your younger self

Dearest ███████

So you find yourself sitting in that place once again, this makes me feel very sad but on the other hand. I know you are safe, And know your eating and sleeping also it stops me worrying about recieving that dreaded phone call that ███████ has been found dead.

I deeply wish you could find another way of replacing that comfort your looking for. your such a lovely woman with so much to give your happy smile and energy that brightnes up any room, however I know that deep pain you carry. almost so deep its buried. I hope that pain can be released so you can shine fully like the star you are. Prison is not the place for you, your too gentle for it really. So i'm sending you some warmth to ~~ease~~ comfort you. even if it's a just for a while.

i'm always here.
when your ready.

Dear ▓▓▓▓ I hope you are doing well, I hope

you will do your sentence and then move on with your life as there is so much more to life.

I have found the most brilliant place for you to go, once you come home.

It's called Clean break its a theatre company and I know you have always wanted to be an actor and with this place you could achieve your dream

Explain prison to a child

You go to prison if you have done something wrong.

Its a place where you go and they lock you in and you can't come home whenever you want to.

You know like repunzel when her fake mum locks her in and the prince saves her its a bit like that but Theres no prince to **save you.**

The little girl and
her friends.

Dearest.

Once upon a time there was a little
girl and she liked to play with her
friends. When they got older she fell
in love with a handsome boy and
wanted to do everything with him.

Not everything he did was good,
but since she loved him, she thought
it was better to be with him doing
naughty things than just to be a good
girl.

Unfortunately, one day, one of her
friends got caught being naughty and
told the police she did naughty things
too.

The police went to her house +
took her to the police station + told
her to tell them the truth or they
would arrest the boy she loved too.
So she told them some of the naughty things
she did and the judge told her to wait
in jail until they could believe she
would be good again.

She met some very interesting and
talented people there, saw a lot
of unfairness and ate a lot of
horrible food.

When they let her come out, the
boy she loved was not very well and
was still doing naughty things,

103

Write Stacey and Deborah into
a tabloid version of *Thelma and Louise*

Breaking News

Killer Women

2 women from London shot and killed
an Innocent man today and went on to
to ~~de~~ Violently Rob Petrol Garages

These women are armed and
dangerous please do not approach

Its seems ~~married~~ woman Deborah Pearson
was cheek to cheek with The Victim, It
Seems he was her Lover and Stacey
gregg (Waitress) ~~he~~ shot him for No
Reason at all, There

STACEY & DEBORAH
ON

SEX DUO KILL INNOCENT FATHER OF THREE ON DRINK-FUELLED NIGHT CLUB BINGE.

~~After a th~~

Witnesses saw Deborah dancing cheek to cheek ~~at Morriens e Grovers~~ ~~whilst~~ her husband was ~~looking~~ working ~~night shifts~~. The waitress, on being questioned, claimed the women 'weren't the murdering type' — however DNA evidence found at the scene pinpoints

the pair as the killers of father of three — shocked Husband of killer, Robbie Murphy says 'I've always loved her + given every thing she's asked for. I can't believe this has happened. I blame it on Stacey, who I've always thought was a bad influence. Police have warned the public not to approach those dangerous individuals.

I Remember

I remember a ashtray.

I remember a wardrobe with no hangers or no door

I rember a metal bed

I remember brown sheets and a green blanket

I remember a harsh top sheet.

I remember a wash basin

I remember a pack of cards.

I remember notice boards.

I remember 4 more other beds opposite.

I remember a fruit bowl.

I remember toiletries.

I remember tabacco.

I wanted to get out.

I wanted a girlfriend.

I wanted drugs

I wanted sweets

I wanted whatever I didn't have.

I wanted clothes.

I wanted comfort.

I wanted myself.

I wanted to be liked.

I Remember!!!

Remember - HAVING PLENTY OF FOOD

Remember = HAVING PLENTY TO DRINK

Remember = HAVING WAY TO MUCH CLOTHES.

Remember - HAVING PICTURES ON MY WALLS

Remember = HAVING TROUBLE SETTLING

Remember - HAVING PLENTY OF TEARS.

" HAVING CIGARETTE

" HAVING ROLLING TABBACO E RIZLA

" HAVING TO MANY MIRRORS.

" HAVING TO PUT UP WID MY PAD MATE

Remember = TRYING HERION

Remember - IT BEEN BEST SLEEP OVER

Remember = BEEN INSIDE

I WANTED

I WANTED = MY CHILDREN.

" = MY FREEDOM.

I WANTED - NOT TO BE LOCKUP

I WANTED =

OUT!!!

List your memories / clichés of prison

- inmate having affair with gym officer
- ~~prison~~ ~~woman~~ found beat up in the shower
- file hidden in a cake
  botch
- prison dyke~~s~~ running wing
- junkie prisoner running errands
- shit parcels thrown out of window
- rats + cockroaches
- ⅠⅠ⊦⊦ days written out on wall
  in roman numerals
- bread + water diet
- 'get yer 'ead down → do your bird'.
- passing drugs/money etc on visits
- escape over wall

pussy sucking.

fighting over chicks

De-crutching | shitting | choccing.

spit in food.

relationship between officer and imate

drugs.

self harm. for attention.

suicide

dirty protest.

bullying.

top dog.

escaping.

obsconding.

drop ne soap.

rape.

peter theif.

picking up butts (scooping).

smoking tea bags.

knicker on radiator.

depression | mental health

1. Bullying
2. Pretty Girl
3. Lesbians
4. Drugs
5. Horrible People
6. Horrible Food
7. Tracksuits
8. Trendy
9. No TV
10. Better than I thought
11. Guilty
12. OITNB
13. Taboo
14. Don't Drop the Soap
15. Bag in @ Visits
16. Prisoners' Wives
17. Women raping women
18. Holiday Camp
19. Inmate having an affair
20. Prisoner beat up in shower

21. Phone in Cake.
22. Butch prison dyke running ring
23. Rats + Cockroaches
24. Days like roman numerals
25. Bread and water diet
26. Passing drugs on visits.
27. Escaping prison.
28. Pussy Sucking
29. fighting over chicks
30. swallowing + shitting out
31. Spitting in Food
32. Drugs   Decratching.
33. Suicide
34. Peter Thief - stealing from eachother's cell.
35. Picking up cigarette butts. (scoopy.
36. Depression + Mental Health
37. Knickers on Radiators

1. Bullying
2. Pretty Girl
3. Lesbians
4. Drugs
5. Horrible People
6. Misery
7. Track suits or Jump Suits
8. Horrible Food
9. TRADING
10.

WWW.OBERONBOOKS.COM